JS

MADTAIL, MI[NIWHALE AND]
OTHER SHAPE POE[MS]

What is a 'madtail, miniwhale'? It's actually a description of a
tadpole in Judith Nicholls's amazing shape poem on the sub-
ject of tadpoles — just one of the extraordinary visual and
verbal delights in Wes Magee's anthology of shape poems.
Covering a wide range of themes and including such poets as
Colin West, George MacBeth and Guillaume Apollinaire, this
is an enjoyable and accessible poetry book with a difference.

Wes Magee is head of a large primary school near Leeds and
is well known for his many poetry anthologies for children. He
also lectures and teaches poetry to both children and adults.

for
Barbara and Michael Hardcastle

MADTAIL, MINIWHALE AND OTHER SHAPE POEMS

Chosen by Wes Magee

Illustrated by
Caroline Crossland

PUFFIN BOOKS

PUFFIN BOOKS

Published by the Penguin Group
Penguin Books Ltd, 27 Wrights Lane, London W8 5TZ, England
Penguin Books USA Inc., 375 Hudson Street, New York, New York 10014, USA
Penguin Books Australia Ltd, Ringwood, Victoria, Australia
Penguin Books Canada Ltd, 10 Alcorn Avenue, Toronto, Ontario, Canada M4V 3B2
Penguin Books (NZ) Ltd, 182–190 Wairau Road, Auckland 10, New Zealand

Penguin Books Ltd, Registered Offices: Harmondsworth, Middlesex, England

First published by Viking Kestrel 1989
Published in Puffin Books 1991
9 10 8

The Acknowledgements on pages 107–8 constitute an extension
of this copyright page.

Printed in England by Clays Ltd, St Ives plc
Filmset in Trump

CONTENTS

ME…AND AMANDA

HOW MY HEART POUNDS!

MADTAIL, MINIWHALE

GOING PLACES

PUSH AND SHOVE...FOXGLOVE

GAME!

WHY DOES A FLY?

OLD BILL BONES

RIPPLES AND RAIN

ME...
AND
AMANDA

ME AND AMANDA

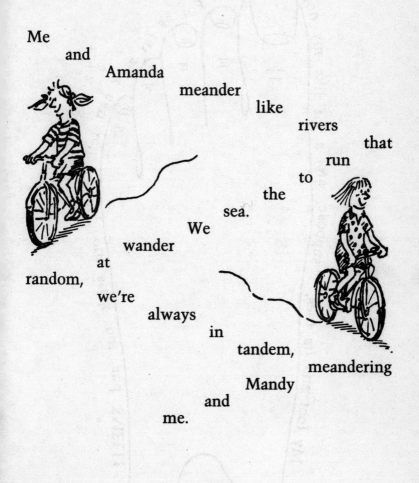

Me
   and
      Amanda
         meander
            like
              rivers
                 that
               run
             to
         the
      sea.
     We
   wander
 at
random,
we're
  always
    in
      tandem,
         meandering
     Mandy
   and
  me.

COLIN WEST

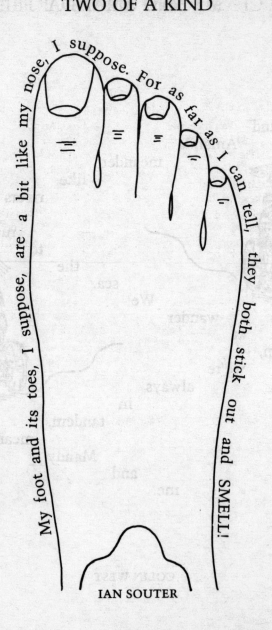

My foot and its toes, I suppose, are a bit like my nose, I suppose. For as far as I can tell, they both stick out and SMELL!

IAN SOUTER

THE CLASSROOM CIRCLE OF FRIENDS

and I like Anne
Van likes me　　→ I like Anne
Dee likes Van　　Anne likes Wayne
Titch likes Dee　　Wayne likes Raj
Del likes Titch　　Raj likes Shane
Mitch likes Del　　Shane likes Paul
Ray likes Mitch　　Paul likes Pam
Lai likes Ray　　Pam likes Shaz
George likes Lai　　Shaz likes Sam
Thai likes George　　Sam likes Parv
Faye likes Thai　　Parv likes Jo
Seth likes Faye　　Jo likes Mick
Chris likes Seth　　Mick likes Mo
Beth likes Chris　　Mo likes Val
Ken likes Beth　　Val likes Jill
Phil likes Ken　　Jill likes Trish
Trish likes Phil

WES MAGEE

[→ start here]

HEART

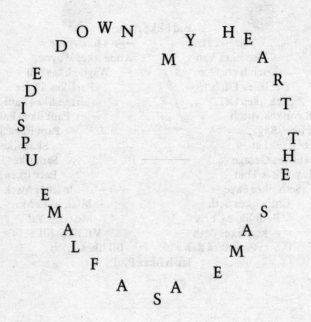

GUILLAUME APOLLINAIRE

THE UPSIDE-DOWN FROWN

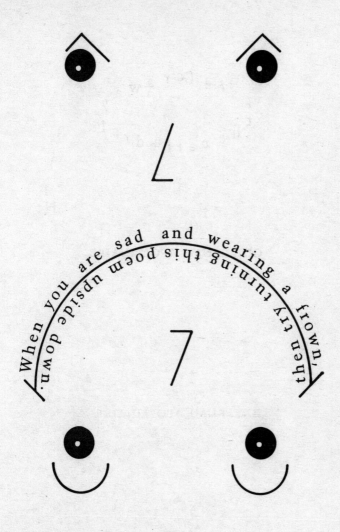

When you are sad and wearing a frown, then try turning this poem upside down.

IAN SOUTER

I SEE

I see far away
the cathedral

GUILLAUME APOLLINAIRE

DON'T SAY A WORD

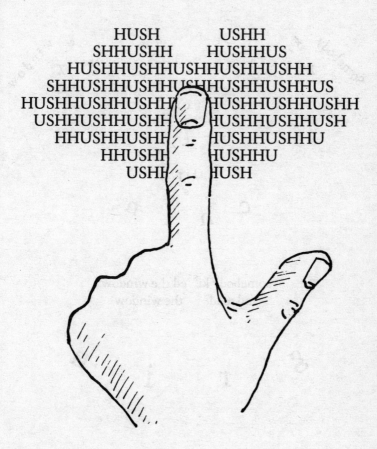

```
        HUSH          USHH
       SHHUSHH      HUSHHUS
    HUSHHUSHHUSHHUSHHUSHH
   SHHUSHHUSHHUSHHUSHHUSHHUS
HUSHHUSHHUSHH      HUSHHUSHHUSHH
 USHHUSHHUSHH      HUSHHUSHHUSH
   HHUSHHUSHH      HUSHHUSHHU
     HHUSHH        HUSHHU
      USHH          HUSH
```

ANNE ENGLISH

SOMEBODY KISSED THE WINDOW

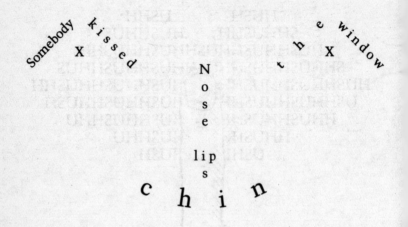

Somebody x kissed t h e x window

Nose
lips
c h i n

somebody ki^{ss}ed the window
and made   the window

g   r   i   n

GINA DOUTHWAITE

SPAGHETTI

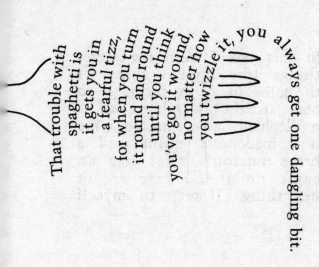

That trouble with spaghetti is it gets you in a fearful tizz, for when you turn it round and round until you think you've got it wound, no matter how you twizzle it, you always get one dangling bit.

One day I'll follow all the bends until I've found a pair of ends.

NOEL PETTY

IN THIS BOX

In this box I keep my secret
things like foreign coins wi
th holes in   them, a ru
bber in the   shape of a
n elephant, a   thimble whic
h is made of   china and a
brass button   that has an
eagle on it.   There are ot
her things I keep to myself

JOHN FAIRFAX

HOW
MY
HEART
POUNDS!

BALLOON

as
big   as
ball as round
as sun . . . I tug
and pull you when
you run and when
wind blows I
say polite
ly
H
O
L
D
M
E
T
I
G
H
T
L
Y.

COLLEEN THIBAUDEAU

25

CHILD SKIPPING

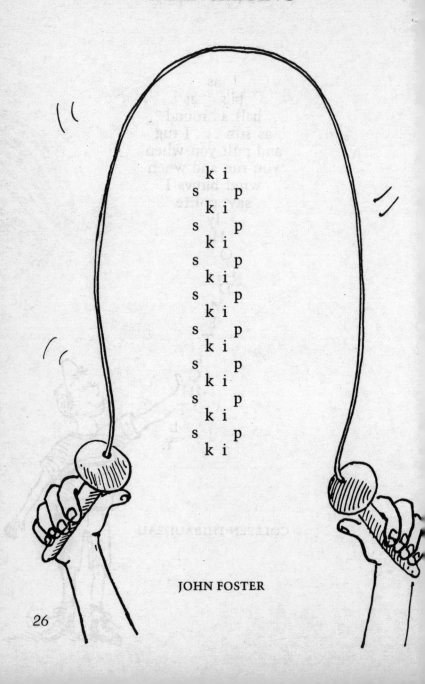

s k i p
s k i p
s k i p
s k i p
s k i p
s k i p
s k i p
s k i p
s k i p
s k i p
k i

JOHN FOSTER

POGO STICK

Upon my pogo stick I pounce
And out of school I homeward bounce.

I bounce so high, how my heart pounds
Until at last I'm out of bounds.

COLIN WEST

ROPE

R
O
P
E
R
O
P
E
R
O
P
E
R
O
P
E
R
O
P
E
R
O
P
E

PETER THABIT JONES

HOW TO DIVE

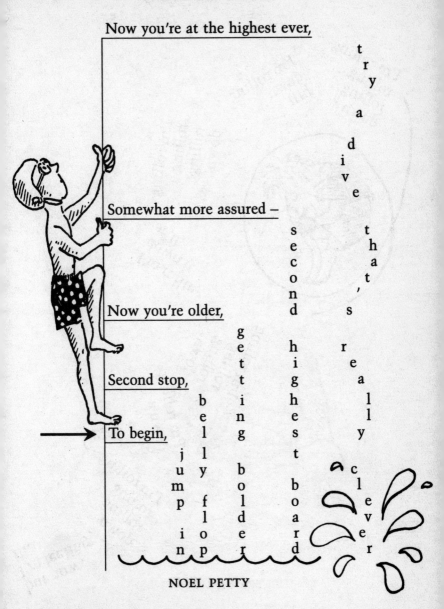

Now you're at the highest ever,   try a dive that's really clever

Somewhat more assured –   second highest board

Now you're older,   getting bolder

Second stop,   belly flop

To begin,   jump in

NOEL PETTY

ROLLING DOWN A HILL

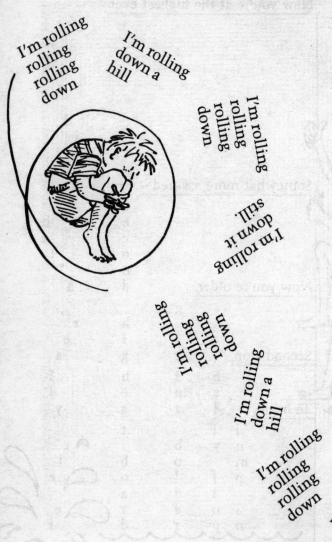

I'm rolling
rolling
rolling
down

I'm rolling
down a
hill

I'm rolling
rolling
rolling
down

I'm rolling
down it
still.

I'm rolling
rolling
rolling
down

I'm rolling
down a
hill

I'm rolling
rolling
rolling
down

but now
I'm feeling
ill.

COLIN WEST

DIZZY

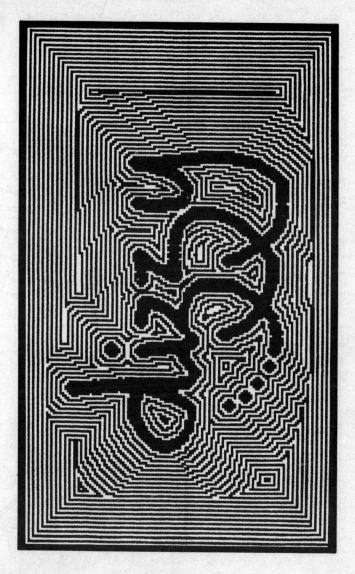

IAN LARMONT

A CELLO

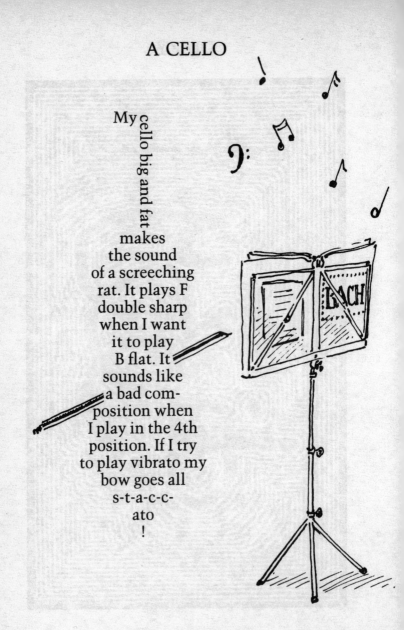

My cello big and fat
makes
the sound
of a screeching
rat. It plays F
double sharp
when I want
it to play
B flat. It
sounds like
a bad com-
position when
I play in the 4th
position. If I try
to play vibrato my
bow goes all
s-t-a-c-c-
ato
!

RICHARD LESTER

MADTAIL,
MINIWHALE

FROGSPAWN

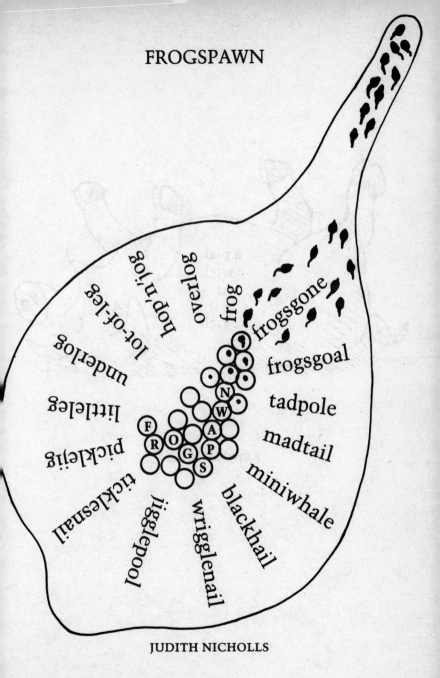

frogsgone
frogsgoal
tadpole
madtail
miniwhale
blackhail
wrigglenail
jigglepool
ticklesnail
picklejig
littleleg
underlog
lot-of-leg
hop'n'jog
overlog
frog

FROGSPAWN

JUDITH NICHOLLS

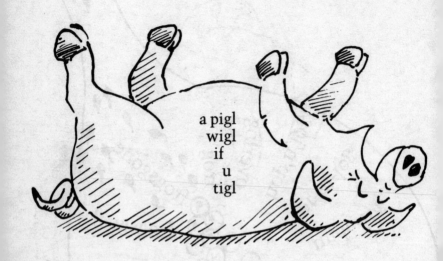

a pigl
wigl
if
u
tigl

ARNOLD SPILKA

SISTERS

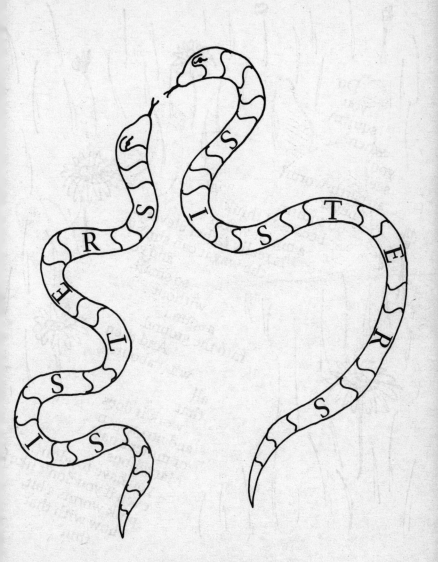

GINA DOUTHWAITE

EARTH-WORM

Do
you
squirm
when
you
see
an earth-worm?
    I never
        do squirm
            because I think
                a big fat worm
                    is really rather clever
                        the way it can shrink
                                and go
                            so small
                        without
                    a sound
                into the ground.
                            And then
                        what about

            all
                that
                    work it does
                        and no oxygen
                            or miner's hat?
                        Marvellous
                            you have to admit,
                                even if you don't like f
                                    pink worms a bit,
                                        how with that
                                            thin

slippery skin
it makes its way
day after day
through the soil,
such honest toil.
And don't forget
the dirt
it eats, I bet
you wouldn't like to come out
at night to squirt
it all over the place
with no eyes in your face:
I doubt
too if you know
an earth-worm is deaf, but
it can hear YOU go
to and fro
even if you cut
it in half.
So
do not laugh
or squirm
again
when
you
suddenly
see
a worm.

LEONARD CLARK

39

THREE BLIND MICE

three blind mice a carving knife did ever you see such fun in your life as three blind mice see how they run they all run after the farmer's wife she cuts off their tails with

IAN LARMONT

GOING
PLACES

OVERTAKING

```
acar              avan acaravan
             acar avan acaravan
             avan acar acaravan
             avan acar acaravan
             avan acar acaravan
             avan acaravan acar
             avan acaravan        acar
```

IAN LARMONT

MOTORWAY

beneath me
where I stand on the bridge
like the captain
of an ocean-going liner

w   s
a   e
v   a
e   o
        f   s
u   o
p   t   u
o   r   n
n   a   d
        f
w   f
a   i
v   c
e

wave upon wave — of traffic — sea sound

coaches, caravans, lorries, cars,
container waggons, land rovers,

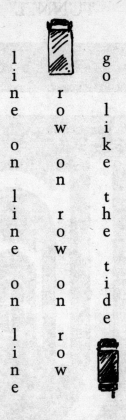

line
on
line
on
line

row
on
row
on
row

go
like
the
tide

never ending,
never ending.

JOAN POULSON

TUNNEL

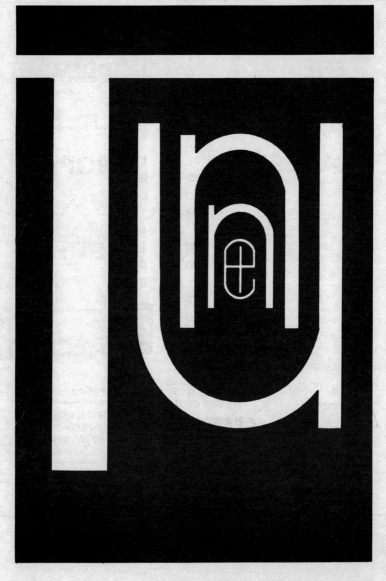

STANLEY COOK

DEVELOPMENT

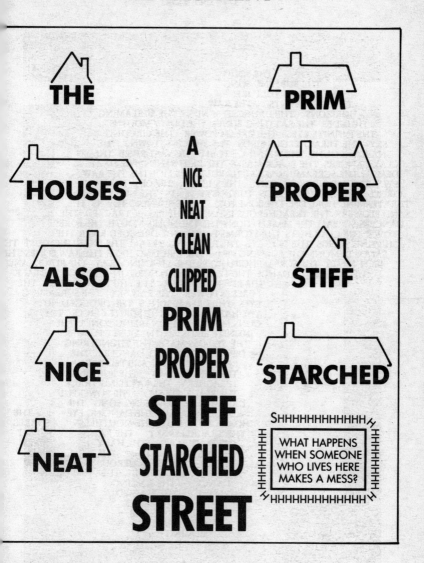

THE

PRIM

HOUSES

PROPER

ALSO

STIFF

NICE

STARCHED

NEAT

A
NICE
NEAT
CLEAN
CLIPPED
PRIM
PROPER
STIFF
STARCHED
STREET

SHHHHHHHHHHHHHH

WHAT HAPPENS
WHEN SOMEONE
WHO LIVES HERE
MAKES A MESS?

HHHHHHHHHHHHH

ROBERT FROMAN

AFRICA

THE SONG
THE BURNING SONG
THE DEMON VULTURES
THE HAZY TENTS   THE RAW
HORIZONS   THE DRUGGED SANDS   THE SCREAMING
THUNDER THE RATTLING BONES THE DUSTY MOUTHS
THE INFINITE EYES   THE DREAM POWER   THE CIRCLING
SKY THE TREACHEROUS BIRDS THE SHIFTING TOWNS THE
SNARLING GUNS THE BURNING STORM THE VAST RIVER THE
CLAY DANCERS THE BLACK MASKS THE RICH SANDS THE HAZY
DEMON THE SCREAMING SKIES THE VULTURES MOUTHS THE RAW
EYES THE THUNDEROUS SONG THE SHIFTING TRACKS THE VAST
CIRCLE THE RATTLING BIRDS THE DUSTY TENTS THE GUNS SNARL
THE STEAMING HORIZON THE BONE FOREST THE BURNING TOWNS THE
SAND FLOWERS THE TREACHEROUS INFINITE THE BLACK TRACKED THE
DANCERS SCREAM THE MASKED GUNS THE THUNDERS MOUTH THE FOREST
TOWN THE CLAY HUTS THE STORMS POWER THE DRUGGED RIVER THE
SHIFTING SONGS THE SKYS EYE THE RATTLING DREAM THE SNARLING DUST TH
SANDS DEMONS THE BURNING BIRDS THE CIRCLING HAZE THE RAW BONES THE
RICH TENTS   THE SCREAMING FLOWER THE STEAMING CLAY THE BLACK SAND
THE MASKED   DANCE THE TREACHEROUS HORIZON THE STORMS TRACK
THE RIVER THUNDER   THE SHIFTY VULTURES   THE
FORESTS POWER   THE RAW SKY   THE SCREAMING
EYES THE DREAM SONGS THE DRUGGED HUTS
THE HAZY TOWNS   THE BURNT CIRCLE   THE
GUNS MOUTH THE SNARLING BONES THE
INFINITE BIRDS   THE DUSTY FLOWERS
THE STORMS MASK THE THUNDERING
DEMONS   THE TENT DANCERS   THE
RICH CLAY   THE SHIFTED POWER
THE SANDY RIVER   THE BURNING
TREACHERY THE RATTLING TRACK
THE BLACK STEAM   THE POWERFUL
DREAM THE FLOWERING SONG THE
DRUGGED SCREAM THE DANCING EYE   THE
HORIZONTAL HUT THE MOUTHLESS   SNARLS
THE TRACKLESS SKY   THE RAW   FOREST
THE TENT TOWN   THE HAZY   RIVER
THE INFINITE SHIFT   THE   BIRD
STORM   THE TREACHEROUS   DEMON
THE BURNING DRUG   THE   GUN
DANCE   THE SINGING
BONE   THE MASKED
RICH   THE BLACK
CIRCLING   THE
VAST DREAM
SINGING

DAVE CALDER

48

5

4

3

2

1 rocket

2 the moon

3 flew it

what 4 ?

5

4

3

2

1 rocket

MICHAEL ROSEN

THE NASTIES ROCKET

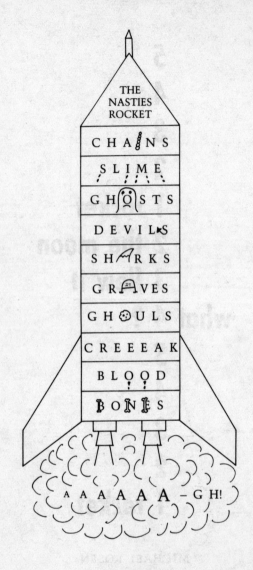

DAVID HORNER

OUR CLASS ROCKET

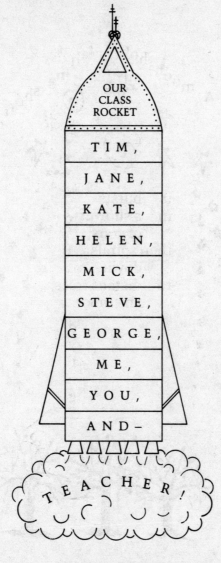

OUR
CLASS
ROCKET

TIM,

JANE,

KATE,

HELEN,

MICK,

STEVE,

GEORGE,

ME,

YOU,

AND –

TEACHER!

DAVID HORNER

GIANT ROCKET

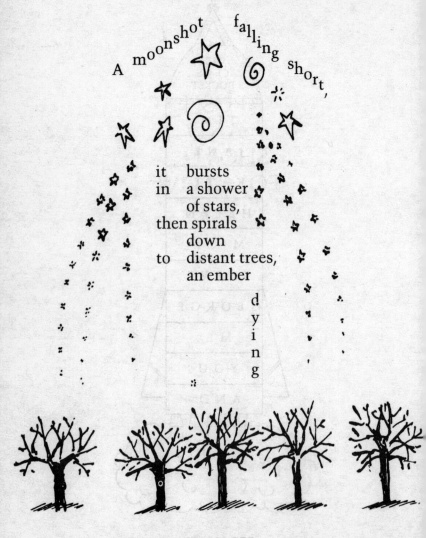

A moonshot falling short,

it   bursts
in   a shower
       of stars,
then spirals
       down
to   distant trees,
       an ember

               d
               y
               i
               n
               g

WES MAGEE

PUSH
AND
SHOVE...
FOXGLOVE

(to be read from the bottom)

FOXGLOVE

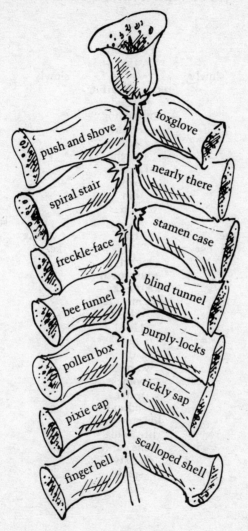

push and shove
foxglove

spiral stair
nearly there

freckle-face
stamen case

bee funnel
blind tunnel

pollen box
purply-locks

pixie cap
tickly sap

finger bell
scalloped shell

SUE COWLING

SPRINGBURST

(to be read from the bottom)

FLOWER!
the

slowly   slowly

the petal curling
the bud,
awakening.
Oh, the
up!
straight
I know!
Now
hm.
hm

see.   see.

me   Hm   me

Let   Let

higher…
must reach
for the sky –
Now, must reach
I be!
I live!
up
tip
warmth
coolness
water,
food and
life growing,
life, being,
in the dark –
(seed style)
spark
A

JOHN TRAVERS MOORE

TREE

STANLEY COOK

IN THE WOODS

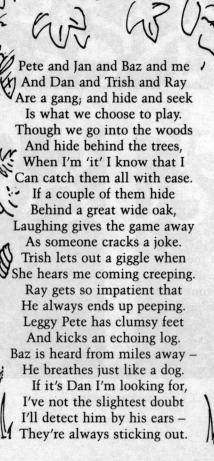

Pete and Jan and Baz and me
And Dan and Trish and Ray
Are a gang; and hide and seek
Is what we choose to play.
Though we go into the woods
And hide behind the trees,
When I'm 'it' I know that I
Can catch them all with ease.
If a couple of them hide
Behind a great wide oak,
Laughing gives the game away
As someone cracks a joke.
Trish lets out a giggle when
She hears me coming creeping.
Ray gets so impatient that
He always ends up peeping.
Leggy Pete has clumsy feet
And kicks an echoing log.
Baz is heard from miles away –
He breathes just like a dog.
If it's Dan I'm looking for,
I've not the slightest doubt
I'll detect him by his ears –
They're always sticking out.

Behind
A birch
Jan tries
To press.
It's far
Too slim
To hide
Her dress.

So when a tell-
tale sign I find
I know someone
Is there behind.
It could be Ray,
It could be Dan,
It could be Baz,
Or Trish or Jan.
I creep up soft
And tiger-like,
Then just as I'm
About to strike
A horrid thought
Can make me jump
And make my heart
Go bump-bump-bump
And make my hair
Stand on my head:
What if it's some-
thing else instead?

NOEL PETTY

LITTLE ACORNS

if the oaks tell jokes
if the palm can sing a psalm
if the elm excels at villanelles
if the ash can bash out a sonnet
if the sycamore cares for metaphor
if the weeping-willow trees like similes
if the chestnut's nuts about raps and chants
if the pines and the limes write lines that rhyme
if the hickory's trick is the limerick
if the yew does a cool haiku or clerihew
if the plane can scribble a cinquain
if the apple counts in syllables
if the firs prefer free verse
if the plum makes puns
THEN
LET
THIS
BE MY
POETREE

DAVID HORNER

GAME!

CRICKET...8 FOR 1

boundary
boundary

blockhole bungle OWZAT!

bat
bat
bat
bat
bat

ball
ball
ball
bouncer
beamer

bowler
bowler
bowler
bowler
bowler
bowler

IAN LARMONT

PING-PONG

Swatted between bats
The celluloid ball
Leaps on unseen elastic
Skimming the taut net.

Sliced		Spun
Screwed		Cut
Dabbed		Smashed
	Point	
	Service	
Ping		Pong
Pong		Ping
Bing		Bong
Bong		Bing
	Point	
	Service	
Ding		Dong
Dong		Ding
Ting		Tong
Tang		Tong
	Point	
	Service	
Angled		Slipped
Cut		Driven
Floated		Caressed
Driven		Hammered
	THWACKED	
	Point	

Service

Bit	Bat
Tip	Tap
Slip	Slap
Zip	Zap
Whip	Whap

Point
Service

Left	Yes
Right	Yes
Twist	Yes
Skids	Yes
Eighteen	Seventeen
Eighteen	All
Nineteen	Eighteen
Nineteen	All
Twenty	Nineteen

Point
Service

Forehand	Backhand
Swerves	Yes
Rockets	Yes
Battered	Ah
Cracked	Ah

Smashed

Smashed

SMASHED

GAME

GARETH OWEN

CUP FINAL

T. O'Day

W. E. March   T. O. G. Lory

J. Usty   O. Uwait   N. See

G. O'Dow

A. Day   W. Ewill   N. Infa   H. I. Story

Young   N. Fast   M. O'Reskill   I. T. Sreally

W. Egot

A. L. L. Sewnup W. E. Rethel A. D. S. Whollrun

A. Round   W. Embley

W. I. Thecup

ROGER MCGOUGH

WORLD CUP

PAUL HIGGINS

DOWNHILL RACER

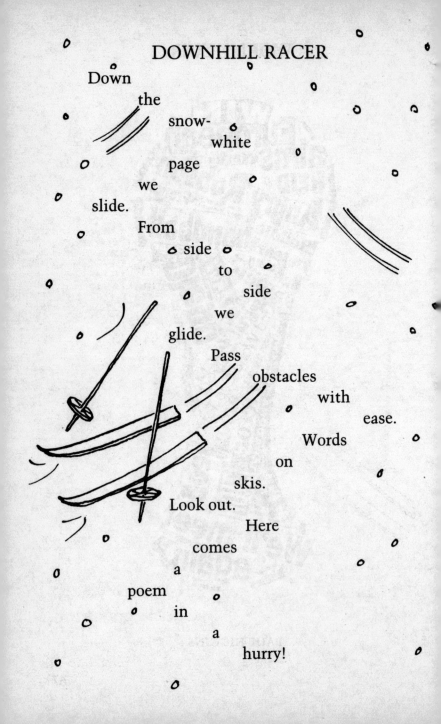

Down
the
snow-
white
page
we
slide.
From
side
to
side
we
glide.
Pass
obstacles
with
ease.
Words
on
skis.
Look out.
Here
comes
a
poem
in
a
hurry!

UPHILL CLIMB

Wheeeeeee

Three
Two
One
go.
another
have
to
top
the
to
back
way
the
all
climb
the
is
part
boring
only
The

ROGER McGOUGH

JACOB'S JUMP

When Jacob, keen to prove his fitness,
Announced he'd jump a chasm,
We gathered round this feat to witness,
With wild enthusiasm.
But Jacob's jump proved so pathetic,
Our hopes have all been banished.
No more he'll try to be athletic,
Since
   d
    o
     w
      n
       t
       h
       e
        v
        o
        i
        d
         h
         e
          v
          a
          n
           i
           s
            h
            e
            d.

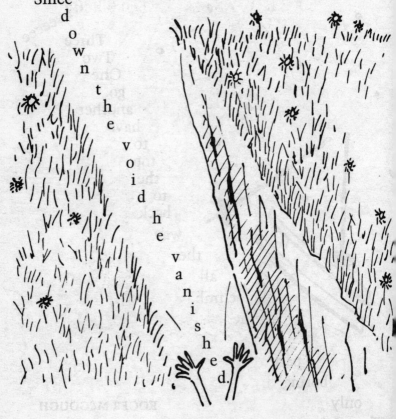

COLIN WEST

WEIGHTLIFTING

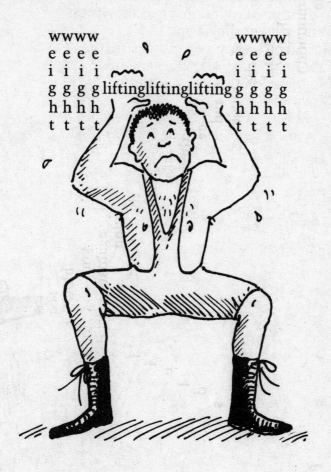

```
wwww                          wwww
e e e e                       e e e e
i i i i                       i i i i
g g g gliftingliftinglifting g g g g
h h h h                       h h h h
t t t t                       t t t t
```

PETER THABIT JONES

CLIMB THE MOUNTAIN

Climb
the
climb
mountain
high,
touch
the
clouds
and
see
the
sky.
Feel
the
wind
against
you
blow, t
h
e
see
f
i
e
l
d
s
f
a
r
f
a
r below

WES MAGEE

WHY
DOES
A
FLY?

ON THE DOORSTEP

on the doorstep
in a brief autumn sun
    a beetle z
          i
         g
          z
        a
        g
      z
        i
         g
        z
      a
      g
      s by
    its black back blazing

JOHN RICE

THE SPIDER'S WEB

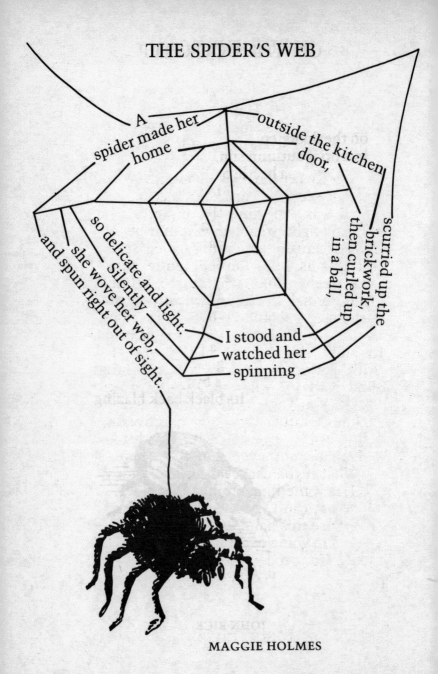

A spider made her home outside the kitchen door,

scurried up the brickwork, then curled up in a ball,

so delicate and light.
Silently she wove her web,
and spun right out of sight.

I stood and watched her spinning

MAGGIE HOLMES

INSIDE THE EGG

Hello,
Goodness me,
I seem to be laid.
It happened too fast
To be shocked or afraid.
It seems a very poky place;
I was expecting lots of space
And light, whatever that may be,
So I can do something called *see*.
If this is Life, I'm not quite sure
It's livelier than what came before.
And, though I've got no wish to moan,
I thought I wouldn't live quite alone.
I've not lost heart, I'm not dejected,
It's just less grand than I expected.
Still, better make the best of things
And wait for what the future brings.
At least it's warm. It could be worse,
Though rather small for a universe.
But wait – I've got a bright idea –
Perhaps not everything's in here.
What if the darkness far and wide
Has something on the other side?
What can I try it with? Suppose
I use this hard bit on my nose?
I'm going to extend my neck
To prod away at it –
Peck! Peck!

NOEL PETTY

LARK

spi
nni
ng
at
the
pe
ak
of
an
inv
isi
ble
je
t
o
f
w
ate
r.
You
bu
rn
a b
lac
k s
tar
at
th
e h
ear
t o
f t
he
blu
e a
ppl
e
c
all
sk
y.
LARK

GEORGE MACBETH

78

EASY DIVER

Pigeon on the roof.

Dives.

Go-

ing

fa-

st. G

O

I

N

G

T

O

HIT HARD!

$^{O}p_{e}{}_{n}{}_{s}$ $_{w}i^{n}g^{s}.$

Softly,   *gently,*

down.

ROBERT FROMAN

I'm only a number two but I act like a swan

SUE STEWART

INVASION

WITH THE FIRST
THE GULLS
EDGE OF LIGHT
CAME BEATING IN
FROM THE SEA
OVER

THE FARMLAND INTO
BIN COUNTRY, WAKING THE
TOWN
ROOFCOUNTRY, DUST-

FROM ITS SUNDAY
MORNING BED THEY
FILLED THE AIR WITH THE
SCREAMS

F THEIR DISSENSION,
SKY WITH THEIR
STRONG
ARROGANT
FILLED THE PALE

WINGS, WHEELING AND
WEAVING THEY BUILT
A TOWERING PATTERN OF FLIGHT
ABOVE THE
TOWN.

PAMELA GILLILAN

TELEPHONE WIRES

JACQUELINE BROWN

OLD
BILL
BONES

PEOPLE

STANLEY COOK

THE LOLLIPOP LADY

When
we come to the
busy street we stand
beside the kerb and wait.
The lady with the lollipop
makes the teatime traffic stop.
When it's our turn to go across
even the hugest lorries pause.
Her lolly's like a magic wand –
cars, bicycles and buses stand
and wait until we're over on
the other pavement. Once
we're gone the traffic
all begins to flow
but only

w
h
e
n

s
h
e

s
i
g
n
a
l
s

GO!

PAMELA GILLILAN

OLD BILL BONES

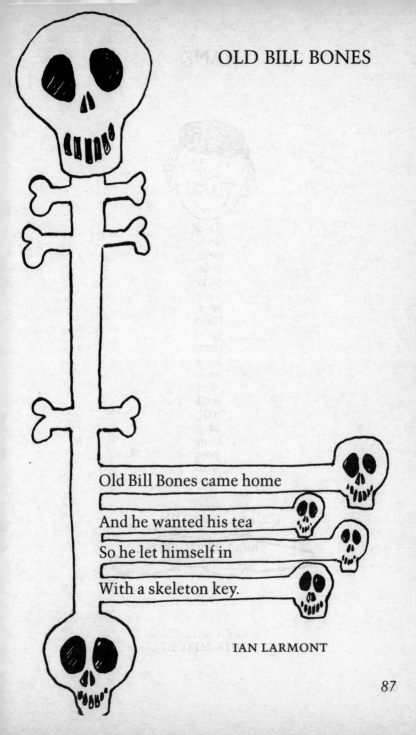

Old Bill Bones came home

And he wanted his tea

So he let himself in

With a skeleton key.

IAN LARMONT

HANK

Thin
as a
bean
pole,
wiry
as a
reed,
Hank
grew
fast
as a
must
-ard
seed,
tall
as a
lamp
post
with
long
flat
feet,
they
call
him Lanky Hanky
down   our   street.

CYNTHIA MITCHELL

WORD PICTURE OF PETER TOMPKINS

The
teacher
said, 'Today
I want you
to draw
me
a lovely picture
of   yourself. It will   be
a   "self-portrait".   If
it   is good I will put   it
on   the wall so I want   to
see   your very best.   OK?'
'I   can't find   a
mirror,' said Peter,
so he looked at
his shadow on the
floor, then he drew
a line   round it
with a   piece of
chalk.   Then he
filled   it with
words.   'This is
a "word   picture"
of Peter,'   he said.

GRAEME AND JENNIFER CURRY

PANTOMIME POEM

'HE'S BEHIND YER!'
chorused the children,
but the warning came too late.

The monster leaped forward
and, fastening its teeth into his neck,
tore off the head.

The body fell to the floor.
'MORE' cried the children
'MORE, MORE, MORE

MORE

MORE

MO

ROGER McGOUGH

RIPPLES
AND
RAIN

WAVE

STANLEY COOK

O MY!

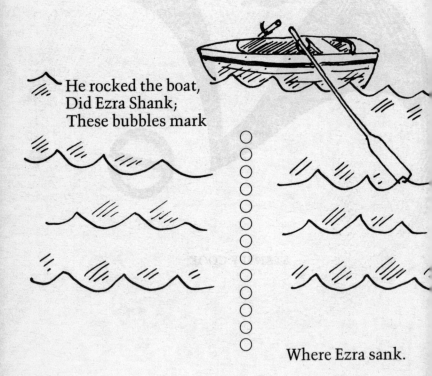

He rocked the boat,
Did Ezra Shank;
These bubbles mark

Where Ezra sank.

ANON.

WHIRLPOOL

IAN LARMONT

A BUTTON

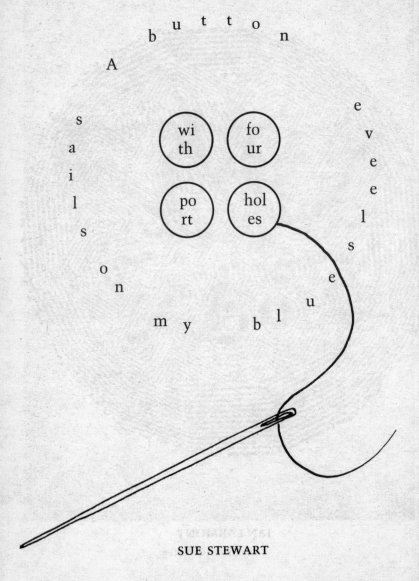

A button
sails
on
my blue
wheels
with four
port holes

SUE STEWART

QUIET SECRET

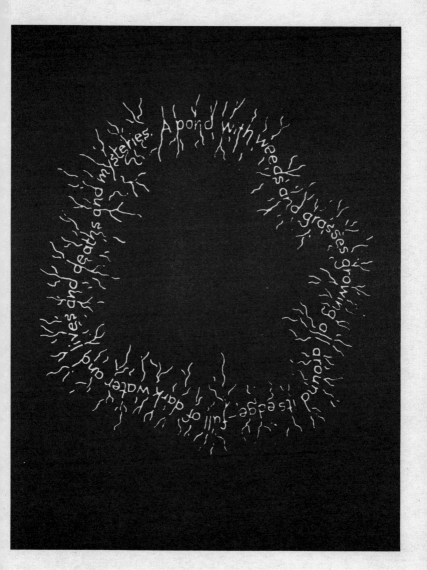

A pond with weeds and grasses growing all around its edge—full of dark water and lives and deaths and mysteries.

ROBERT FROMAN

STANLEY COOK

JUST A PASSING SHOWER

sunshine	sunshine	sunshine
sunshine	sunshine	/////
sunshine	/////	sunshine
/////	sunshine	sunshine
sunshine	sunshine	sunshine

ALAN RIDDELL

SHOWER

fierce
    spring
        rain
            full
            gushing
drab   drain
    steely   grey
      sky   puddled
        umbrellas   street
        held   wellies
cars   high   for
    make   children   feet
      spray   want
        birds   out
          huddle   harassed
rain   away   mothers
  becomes   cats   shout
    drops   lie
      slows   asleep
        and   plants
          stops   drink
          doors   deep
         open
           wide
           people
           step
            outside

MOIRA ANDREW

RAIN

I don't like going out in the

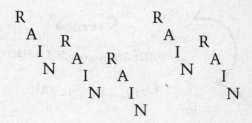

so I bought the biggest

        U   B   R E   L L
              I   A
              N
              T
              H
              E
              W
              O
              R
              L D

PETER THABIT JONES

CLOUDS

Clouds

The white shrouds

Outspread

Overhead

Of ships under sail

Driven by the gale…

Castles in the air…   Icebergs of the sky

The wind's long hair…   Mountainously high…

Suds

The   of foam

gigantic

form   on an airy stream…

of   Piled-up helpings

the thunderstorm…   of soft

ice cream…

Curtains drawn on the sun at noon

or at midnight on the moon…

Arctic archipelago   Banners unfurled

of islands under snow…   Above the world…

STANLEY COOK

FREEZE

The windowsill has grown a beard
      c   c
      i   i
      c   c
      l   l
      e   e

Milk bottles raise their ^{caps}

While puddles cr$_a$ck like broken glass

And trees wear furry w^{rap}s.

SUE COWLING

EVENING STAR

The evening star, a punctual gem, shines like a rajah's maid

GUILLAUME APOLLINAIRE

HOLE POEM

a hole is round and dark and mysterious and silent black and empty and full of

NOTHING

ADRIAN RUMBLE

ACKNOWLEDGEMENTS

The editor and publishers gratefully acknowledge copyright holders for their kind permission to use material in this book.

'Shower' © Moira Andrew, 1989; 'Telephone Wires' © Jacqueline Brown, 1989; 'Traffic Jam Buttie' and 'Africa' © Dave Calder, 1989; 'Earthworm' © the Estate of Leonard Clark, 1975, first published by Dobson Books in *Collected Poems and Verses*; 'Tunnel', 'Tree', 'People', 'Wave', 'Clouds' and 'Pool' © Stanley Cook, 1989; 'Foxglove' and 'Freeze' © Sue Cowling, 1989; 'Word Picture of Peter Tomkins' © Graeme and Jennifer Curry, 1988, first published by Methuen Children's Books Ltd in *Down Our Street*; 'Sisters' and 'Somebody Kissed the Window' © Gina Douthwaite, 1989; 'Don't Say a Word' © Anne English, 1989; 'In This Box' © John Fairfax, 1989; 'Child Skipping' © John Foster, 1989; 'Development', 'Easy Diver' and 'Quiet Secret' © Robert Froman, 1989; 'Invasion' © Pamela Gillilan, 1985, first published by Oxford University Press in *A Fifth Poetry Book*; 'The Lollipop Lady' © Pamela Gillilan, 1987, first published by Oxford University Press in *Another First Poetry Book*; 'World Cup' © Paul Higgins, 1989; 'The Spider's Web' © Maggie Holmes, 1989; 'The Nasties Rocket', 'Our Class Rocket' and 'Little Acorns' © David Horner, 1989; 'Dizzy', 'Three Blind Mice', 'Overtaking', 'Cricket ... 8 for 1', 'Old Bill Bones' and 'Whirlpool' © Ian Larmont, 1989; 'A Cello' © Richard Lester, 1983, first published by Beaver Books in *Poems For Fun*; 'Lark' © George MacBeth, 1973, first published by George Harrap Ltd in *Poemcards*, permission granted by Anthony Sheil Associates; 'Cup Final' © Roger McGough, 1983, first published by Viking Kestrel in *Sky in the Pie*, permission granted by Peters, Fraser & Dunlop; 'Downhill Racer/Uphill Climb' © Roger McGough, 1987, first published by Viking Kestrel in *Nailing the Shadow*, permission granted by Peters, Fraser & Dunlop; 'Pantomime Poem' © Roger McGough, 1971, first published by Jonathan Cape Ltd in *After the Merrymaking*, permission granted by Peters, Fraser & Dunlop; 'The Classroom Circle of Friends', 'Giant Rocket' and 'Climb the Mountain' © Wes Magee, 1989; 'Hank' © Cynthia Mitchell, 1989; 'Frogspawn' © Judith Nicholls, 1985, first published by Faber and Faber in *The*

READ MORE IN PUFFIN

Wouldn't You Like to Know

by Michael Rosen

Down behind the dustbin
I met a dog called Joe.
'What have you got there?' I said.
'Wouldn't you like to know!'

Are you one of those people who think poetry is
soppy? Well, here's a collection of poems by
Michael Rosen that'll change your mind! There
are lots of interesting, funny, silly, sensible,
original and unusual poems for this Puffin
edition – all illustrated by Quentin Blake.

The New Puffin Book of Funny Verse

Edited by Kit Wright

We all know that bicycle
Shortens to bike
So why is an icicle
Never an ike?

Inside this special collection of funny verse, there's a funny bunch of poems that will really make you laugh out loud! There are tales of scrapes at school, some ridiculous animals and even stranger relatives to meet, plus plenty of unbelievable accidents and silly adventures.

With poems from some of the best contemporary writers and a few familiar favourites, this lively and fresh anthology, first published as Funnybunch, is not to be missed.

'Kit Wright has spread his net wider and caught some unexpected goodies' – *Independent on Sunday*

READ MORE IN PUFFIN

For children of all ages, Puffin represents quality and variety – the very best in publishing today around the world.

For complete information about books available from Puffin – and Penguin – and how to order them, contact us at the appropriate address below. Please note that for copyright reasons the selection of books varies from country to country.

On the worldwide web: www.puffin.co.uk

In the United Kingdom: Please write to *Dept. EP, Penguin Books Ltd, Bath Road, Harmondsworth, West Drayton, Middlesex UB7 ODA*

In the United States: Please write to *Consumer Sales, Penguin USA, P.O. Box 999, Dept. 17109, Bergenfield, New Jersey 07621-0120*. VISA and MasterCard holders call 1-800-253-6476 to order Penguin titles

In Canada: Please write to *Penguin Books Canada Ltd, 10 Alcorn Avenue, Suite 300, Toronto, Ontario M4V 3B2*

In Australia: Please write to *Penguin Books Australia Ltd, P.O. Box 257, Ringwood, Victoria 3134*

In New Zealand: Please write to *Penguin Books (NZ) Ltd, Private Bag 102902, North Shore Mail Centre, Auckland 10*

In India: Please write to *Penguin Books India Pvt Ltd, 706 Eros Apartments, 56 Nehru Place, New Delhi 110 019*

In the Netherlands: Please write to *Penguin Books Netherlands bv, Postbus 3507, NL-1001 AH Amsterdam*

In Germany: Please write to *Penguin Books Deutschland GmbH, Metzlerstrasse 26, 60594 Frankfurt am Main*

In Spain: Please write to *Penguin Books S. A., Bravo Murillo 19, 1° B, 28015 Madrid*

In Italy: Please write to *Penguin Italia s.r.l., Via Felice Casati 20, I–20124 Milano*

In France: Please write to *Penguin France S. A., 17 rue Lejeune, F–31000 Toulouse*

In Japan: Please write to *Penguin Books Japan, Ishikiribashi Building, 2–5–4, Suido, Bunkyo-ku, Tokyo 112*

In South Africa: Please write to *Longman Penguin Southern Africa (Pty) Ltd, Private Bag X08, Bertsham 2013*